KENTARO'S

NOODLES

VERTICAL.

Contents

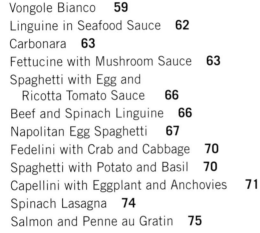
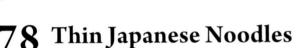

Reference Guide:
Commonly Used Ingredients and Substitutions
Inside back cover

Chinese Noodles

There are two primary kinds of Chinese noodles on the market:
noodles suited to soups and sauces, and steamed noodles for yakisoba.
Gently pull the noodles apart before adding to a pot of boiling water,
then stir them with big, sweeping motions.
Everyone has their own preference when it comes to cooking time,
but I generally cook my noodles a minute or so less than the time listed on the package.
If the package says 3 minutes, I check my noodles after 2.
Usually they are still a little too chewy, but if I plan on simmering them
in soup later on, then that's perfect. If I want to just pour hot broth over my noodles
before serving, about 2 1/2 minutes cooking time will do the trick.
Still, everyone has their own preference. Mushy noodles are a definite no-go, though.
By the way, chilled noodles firm up when soaked in ice water, so cook them until
they're very tender, either by following package directions or cooking a little longer.

Tan Tan
Noodle Soup

**So spicy it will sting your
tongue and steal your heart!**

For a deliciously spicy flavor, sauté Doubanjiang first.
Next cook the meat for a robust flavor.
Add to that fiery Szechuan peppercorns and rich sesame paste.
The result is a scrumptiously complex flavor, easily achieved by using soup mix.
Both soy sauce and miso flavored broths work well.

Tan Tan Noodle Soup

Ingredients (Serves 2)
2 servings Chinese noodles
5 1/4 oz (150 g) ground pork
2 oz (60 g) boiled bamboo shoots
2 shiitake mushrooms
1/2 bunching onion (or green onion or leek)
1/3 bag bean sprouts
1 to 2 Tbsp Szechuan peppercorns (*hua jiao*)
1 to 1 1/2 Tbsp sesame oil
1/2 to 1 Tbsp Doubanjiang (Chinese chili paste)
2 cloves garlic, minced
1 nub ginger, minced
4 Tbsp white sesame paste
2 servings ramen soup mix (soy sauce or miso based)
Chopped spring onions (or scallions)

1 Make Soup

1. Dice bamboo shoots and shiitake mushrooms into 1/5" (5 mm) cubes. Mince bunching onion. Remove root ends of bean sprouts.

2. Lightly sprinkle Szechuan peppercorns with water. This makes it easier to chop them.

3. Coarsely chop peppercorns.

Note
If you store sesame paste upside-down, it's easy to scoop out.

4. Dissolve soup mix according to package directions. Dilute with an additional 1/4 to 1/2 C boiling water.

5. Add sesame oil to a heated pot and sauté Doubanjiang until fragrant.

6. Add bunching onion, garlic and ginger. Sauté on low heat until fragrant.

7. Add ground pork. Stir-fry on high heat, crumbling as you cook.

8. When meat is lightly browned add shiitake, bean sprouts and bamboo shoots. Stir-fry.

2 Prepare Noodles

3 Serve

9. Add sesame paste when bean sprouts are tender. Stir quickly and add Szechuan peppercorns. Stir-fry until fragrant.

10. Pour in diluted soup mix from step 4.

11. Bring water to a rolling boil and add noodles, breaking up any clumps.

12. Stir occasionally.

13. Drain noodles and place in bowls. Pour steaming hot broth from step 10 over noodles and garnish with chopped spring onions.

Chilled Chinese Noodles

Authentic flavor, prepared with ease

Chilled Chinese noodles are a summer favorite, usually sold with dipping sauce included.
The sauce is what makes them delicious, so I've included the recipe so you can enjoy these noodles any time, in any season.

Ingredients (Serves 2)

2 servings Chinese noodles
Sauce:
- 1 C water
- 2 Tbsp rice vinegar
- 1 1/2 Tbsp soy sauce
- 1 1/2 Tbsp oyster sauce
- 1/2 Tbsp sugar

3 slices ham
1 cucumber
1/2 bag bean sprouts
Salt, to taste
Omelet:
- 2 eggs
- Pinch salt
- 1 Tbsp vegetable oil

Red pickled ginger, roasted white sesame seeds and Japanese mustard paste, to taste

1 Mix Sauce

1. Mix together sauce ingredients. Chill in refrigerator, if desired.

2 Prepare Toppings

2. Julienne cucumber and ham.

3. Remove root ends of bean sprouts. Parboil in salted water.

4. Make a thin, crepe-like omelet. Stir salt into lightly beaten eggs. Add vegetable oil to a heated skillet and spread eggs thinly over skillet surface.

5. Remove omelet when cooked through. Cut in half, then into thin strips.

3 Prepare Noodles

6. Bring water to a rolling boil and add noodles. Cook according to package directions.

7. Rinse noodles well.

8. Chill in ice water.

4 Combine and Serve

9. Drain noodles and serve in dishes. Pour on sauce from step 1.

10. Arrange toppings and pickled ginger on top of noodles and sprinkle with sesame seeds. Serve mustard paste on the side.

Bang-Bang Chicken with Noodles

Ground sesame makes for a richly flavored sauce

Potently flavorful sesame sauce combined with the refreshing taste of boiled chicken. Light and luscious, yet rich and delicious.

Ingredients (Serves 2)

2 servings Chinese noodles
2 chicken breasts

A
- 1/2 bunching onion (or green onion) (just the greens)
- 1 clove garlic, halved
- 1 nub ginger, cut into thirds

1 cucumber
1/2 bunching onion

B
- Grated daikon and grated ginger, to taste
- 4 Tbsp ground white sesame seeds
- 3 Tbsp sesame oil
- 1 tsp each salt, sugar, soy sauce and rice vinegar

Salt, to taste

Instructions

1. Add water and mixture A to a soup pot and bring to a boil. Add chicken. Boil until chicken is cooked through to the center. Let chicken cool, then remove skin and shred meat. Peel cucumber, pound lightly, and break into pieces. Mince bunching onion.
2. Combine mixture B in a large bowl. Add chicken, cucumber and bunching onion and mix well. Cook noodles in boiling water, rinse, and chill in ice water. Drain noodles well and add to bowl with sauce. Add salt as needed.

Note
Add salt and soy sauce to leftover chicken broth for a light and refreshing soup.

Spicy Meaty Tan Tan Noodles

Love that tangy taste!

Delicious meaty miso with sweet, sour and spicy sauce, served on top of smooth Chinese noodles. Make sure the sauce is well-chilled. The pairing of hot miso with cool noodles is what makes this dish delicious.

Ingredients (Serves 2)

2 servings Chinese noodles
Sauce:
- 2 1/2 C water
- 3 Tbsp white sesame paste
- 2 to 3 Tbsp ground white sesame seeds
- 2 Tbsp each oyster sauce and rice vinegar
- 1 1/2 Tbsp miso
- 1 Tbsp each sesame oil and soy sauce
- 1 light Tbsp sugar
- 1 to 2 Tbsp Doubanjiang (Chinese chili paste)
- Chili oil, to taste

5 1/4 oz (150 g) ground pork
1/2 bunch garlic chives
1/2 bunching onion (or green onion)
2 cloves garlic
1 nub ginger
1/2 Tbsp sesame oil
1 to 2 Tbsp roasted white sesame seeds
1 Tbsp each sake, soy sauce and oyster sauce
Salt, pepper and chili oil, to taste

Garlic chives are an essential finishing touch.

Instructions

1. Mix sauce ingredients in a bowl and chill well in refrigerator.
2. Chop garlic chives to 2/5" (1 cm) lengths. Mince bunching onion, garlic and ginger.
3. Add sesame oil to a frying pan and sauté bunching onion, garlic and ginger over low heat until fragrant. Add ground pork and season with salt and pepper. Stir-fry, crumbling meat.
4. When meat is browned, add roasted sesame seeds, sake, soy sauce and oyster sauce. Stir well.
5. Boil noodles, rinse, and chill in ice water. Drain. Serve in dishes, top with garlic chives and pour in chilled sauce from step 1. Add a generous amount of meat mixture and sprinkle on chili oil to taste.

Zhajiang Noodles
Flavor with red miso and oyster sauce!

Rich miso-sautéed meat and refreshing vegetables complement each other perfectly in this classic Chinese noodle dish. You can make it without the traditional sweet noodle sauce. Stir well and enjoy.

Ingredients (Serves 2)
2 servings Chinese noodles
7 oz (200 g) ground pork
1 cucumber
2 to 3 leaves lettuce
1/2 bunching onion (or green onion)
1 clove garlic
1 nub ginger

A ⎧ 2 Tbsp water
⎪ 1 1/2 Tbsp each red miso and sugar
⎨ 1 Tbsp each sake and oyster sauce
⎩ 1/2 tsp rice vinegar

1 Tbsp sesame oil

Instructions
1. Mince bunching onion, garlic and ginger. Julienne cucumber and shred lettuce. Combine mixture A.
2. Add sesame oil to a heated pan and sauté garlic and ginger over low heat until fragrant. Add bunching onion and continue sautéing. Add ground pork, raise heat to high, and stir-fry.
3. When meat is browned, pour in mixture A and stir.
4. Cook noodles in boiling water, rinse, and chill in ice water. Drain well and serve in dishes. Top with cucumber, lettuce, and meat.

Thai-style Dressed Noodles

Hot noodles topped with a delectable variety of flavors and textures!

Cook noodles and coat with thick peanut sauce. Garnish with crispy bean sprouts, crunchy peanuts, fresh cilantro and spicy cayenne pepper. It couldn't get any simpler.

Ingredients (Serves 2)

2 servings Chinese noodles
4 to 5 fried round fish cakes (*age-kamaboko*)
   (or sub. imitation crab sticks, sautéed)
1/3 bag bean sprouts
1/4 bunch spring onion (or scallions)
Cilantro, to taste

A ⎡ 1 Tbsp dried shrimp
   ⎣ 1/2 Tbsp each sake and lukewarm water

B ⎡ 1 1/2 Tbsp Nam pla (Thai fish sauce)
  ⎢ 1 Tbsp peanut butter (mince if using the
  ⎢   crunchy kind)
  ⎢ 1 Tbsp oyster sauce
  ⎣ 2 tsp rice vinegar

Buttered peanuts and cayenne pepper, to taste

Instructions

1. Remove root ends of bean sprouts. Chop spring onions and cilantro. Combine mixture A in a small bowl and set aside to reconstitute shrimp. Combine mixture B in a large bowl.
2. Boil noodles and drain well. Add noodles to bowl with mixture B, add mixture A, and stir well. Serve noodles in dishes and top with fried fish cakes, spring onions, bean sprouts and cilantro. Finish with buttered peanuts and cayenne pepper.

Ramen with Tofu

Rich and thick soy-based sauce

Delicious ramen noodles with melt-in-your-mouth tofu. Simply cook the ramen noodle as usual. Unbelievably easy, this combination of soft and tender textures is a delectable delight.

Ingredients (Serves 2)

2 servings ramen noodles
1 block silken tofu
1/3 bundle *komatsuna* (mustard greens. Or sub. spinach)

A ⌈ 1 Tbsp potato (or corn) starch
  ⌊ 2 Tbsp water

B ⌈ Dash grated ginger
  | 1/2 C water
  | 1 1/2 Tbsp oyster sauce
  | Soy sauce, to taste
  ⌊ 2 pinches sugar

2 packages instant ramen noodle soup (soy sauce flavor)
Sesame oil and pepper, to taste

Instructions

1. Cut *komatsuna* to 2" (5 cm) lengths. Combine mixture A.
2. Combine mixture B in a frying pan and bring to a boil. Reduce heat to low and add chunks of tofu with a spoon. Boil for 1 to 2 minutes and turn off heat. Stir mixture A well just before adding to pan. Turn on heat and simmer until sauce thickens.
3. Prepare ramen sauce according to package directions.
4. Cook noodles in boiling water and add *komatsuna* 10 seconds before noodles are done. Serve cooked noodles and *komatsuna* in bowls. Pour sauce from step 3 over noodles and top with tofu from step 2. Sprinkle with sesame oil and pepper.

Before adding starch paste to sauce, mix well.

Tom Yum Ramen
Authentic flavor adds exciting appeal!

For genuine, delicious Thai flavor, use tom yum paste with spices already added. Add lemon, garnish with cilantro, and enjoy.

Ingredients (Serves 2)

2 servings Chinese noodles
4 shrimp
1/2 pack *shimeji* (clamshell) mushrooms
1/3 bunch spring onions (or scallions)
2 cloves garlic
1 nub ginger
1 Tbsp vegetable oil

A
- 1 package tom yum paste
- 3 1/4 C water
- 2 Tbsp sake
- 6 to 8 lemongrass stems
- 4 to 5 slices galangal root
- 10 kieffer lime leaves

Nam pla (Thai fish sauce), to taste
Fried onion (store bought), chopped cilantro and lemon wedge, to taste

Instructions

1. Devein shrimp. Cut about 2/5" (1 cm) off root end of *shimeji* mushrooms and break apart. Cut spring onions into 2" (5 cm) lengths. Mince garlic and ginger.
2. Add oil to a heated soup pot and sauté garlic and ginger on low heat until fragrant. Add shrimp and stir-fry on high heat. When shrimp are cooked add *shimeji* mushrooms. Stir-fry.
3. When *shimeji* are tender stir in mixture A ingredients in listed order. Bring soup to a boil over high heat, then reduce heat to low. Simmer for 15 minutes. Add spring onions and simmer briefly.
4. Cook noodles in boiling water and drain well. Serve noodles in dishes and pour on soup from 3. Garnish with fried onion and cilantro. Serve lemon on the side.

Note
Galangal root (pictured in the lower left of the bowl) is a spice with an aroma that's a combination of ginger and pepper. Kieffer lime leaves are often sold dried. Both are spices commonly used in Thai cuisine and should be available in any large supermarket with a good Asian foods section. Also, check ingredients on the back of the tom yum paste, as they are sometimes included. You can use either fresh or dried lemongrass.

Chinese Chicken Noodle Soup
This simple but savory soup will surprise you!

Just boil chicken slowly and thoroughly.
That's all you need to do to create this unbelievably delicious soup.
The only hard part is patient removal of the foam that floats to the surface.

Ingredients (Serves 2)

2 servings Chinese noodles
2 boneless chicken thighs
1/2 bunching onion (or green onion)
   (white stem)
A ⌈ 1 bunching onion (green leaves)
  | 2 cloves garlic, halved
  ⌊ 1 nub ginger, cut in thirds
4 C water
Salt and pepper, to taste

Instructions

1. Remove fat from chicken and cut into 2/5" (1 cm) strips. Cut white stems of bunching onion to 2" (5 cm) pieces, then quarter lengthwise.
2. Add water, chicken, and mixture A to a pot and bring to a boil. Reduce heat to low and simmer for about one hour, occasionally removing foam. Add salt to taste, aiming for the strong flavor of ramen soup. Remove all ingredients except chicken.
3. In a separate pot, cook noodles one minute less than time indicated by package directions, then add to soup. Add white stems of bunching onion and simmer for 1 minute. Sprinkle with pepper.

Note
- Use large chunks of garlic and ginger and boil slowly to draw out the flavor.
- Leave pan uncovered while simmering and let water evaporate for a denser flavor. Remove foam that floats to the surface for a clear and delicious soup.

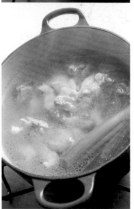

Udon and Soba

Udon (thick wheat noodles) and soba (buckwheat noodles) can be found primarily
in three different forms: fresh, frozen, and dried.
Fresh noodles are sometimes difficult to find, but they have a great texture, flavor and taste.
When cooking fresh noodles, use the package directions as reference and
cook according to your preferred level of doneness.
Sometimes following the directions exactly results in noodles that are too tender.
Dried noodles should be rinsed thoroughly after boiling to wash away any excess starch.
If using the noodles in a soup, it's necessary to reheat them by simmering
in soup stock or dousing with boiling water.
Dried noodles take a little more effort to prepare, but they have an appealing taste,
and they keep well. I personally like to keep them on hand at all times.
Frozen noodles are very easy to use. They cook quickly too.
There is no need to rinse them after boiling, so they can be eaten immediately.
Frozen udon come out consistently firm with a chewy texture.

Curry Udon

Meat makes for a richly flavorful broth!

Curry udon is a popular dish in
Japan and a personal favorite of mine.
I love to eat it and I love to make it.
Stir-fry bunching onion and pork to bring out
their flavors, pour in noodle sauce, and simmer.
Thick udon noodles are a perfect match for this spicy yet soothing soup.

19

Curry Udon

Ingredients (Serves 2)

2 servings udon noodles (frozen)
5 1/4 oz (150 g) pork belly, thinly sliced
1/2 block deep fried tofu (*atsuage*)
1 bunching onion (or green onion)
A [2 to 2 1/2 Tbsp potato (or corn) starch
   3 to 4 Tbsp water
1 Tbsp sesame oil
1 Tbsp curry powder
1 nub ginger, minced
3 1/2 C noodle
   dipping sauce
   (*men tsuyu*),
   diluted to taste
Ground white sesame
   seeds and seven
   spice powder,
   to taste

1. Cut pork into bite-size pieces. Cut deep fried tofu in half from the side and then into 2/5" (1 cm) thick strips. Cut bunching onion to 2 1/2" (6 to 7 cm) pieces then quarter lengthwise. Combine mixture A and stir well.

2. Add sesame oil to a heated pot and stir-fry pork and bunching onion over medium heat.

3. When pork is browned add tofu and stir-fry.

4. When tofu is coated with oil add curry powder. Stir until well blended.

5. Add diluted noodle sauce and ginger.

6. Bring to a boil, then reduce heat to low. Simmer for about 5 minutes, occasionally removing foam that floats to the surface.

7. Turn off heat. Stir mixture A again and add to the pot. Turn on heat and simmer until sauce thickens.

8. Stir in plenty of ground sesame seeds.

9. Cook udon noodles in boiling water.

10. Drain cooked noodles and add to curry soup. Stir well, then serve in bowls. Season with seven-spice powder, if desired.

Curry Soba

Yuzu peel adds a nice accent!

In my opinion, a light, refreshing soup suits soba noodles best. So for soba, simmer ingredients without sautéing first.

Ingredients (Serves 2)

2 servings soba noodles (dried)
1 chicken breast
1 sheet thin fried tofu (*aburaage*)
1/2 bundle scallions
A ⎡ 2 to 2 1/2 Tbsp potato (or corn) starch
⎣ 3 to 4 Tbsp water
3 1/2 C noodle dipping sauce (*men tsuyu*), diluted to taste
1 1/2 Tbsp curry powder
1/2 nub ginger, grated
Yuzu peel (or lemon zest)

1. Slice chicken breast into 1/4" (6 to 7 mm) strips and fried tofu into 2/5" (1 cm) widths. Cut scallions into 2 1/2" (6 to 7 cm) pieces. Combine mixture A and stir well.

2. Bring diluted noodle sauce to a boil, then reduce heat to low. Add curry powder and chicken. Simmer for 7 minutes, occasionally removing foam that floats to the surface.

3. Add fried tofu strips and scallions and simmer for an additional 2 minutes.

4. Turn off heat. Stir mixture A again then add to the pot. Turn on heat and simmer until sauce thickens.

5. Cook soba noodles in plenty of boiling water, then rinse and drain well.

6. Add noodles to soup from step 4. Stir well to reheat noodles. Serve in bowls and garnish with grated ginger and *yuzu* peel as desired.

Lightly Dressed Soba with Mixed Toppings

A fragrant smorgasbord of flavors!

Soft-boiled eggs, *natto*, scallions – anything and everything that goes well with soba noodles. This truly easy dish takes no time and no trouble. Finish with soy sauce and enjoy.

Ingredients (Serves 2)
2 servings soba noodles (dried)
10 *shiso* (or basil or mint) leaves
1 bud Japanese ginger (*myoga*)
1/3 bunch spring onions (or scallions)
1/2 pack daikon seed sprouts (*kaiware*)
1 heaping Tbsp dried *wakame* seaweed
2 packs *natto* (fermented soybeans)
2 soft-boiled eggs
4 Tbsp tempura crumbs (*ten kasu*)
Grated ginger and soy sauce, to taste

1. Mince *shiso* leaves and julienne Japanese ginger. Chop bunching onion. Remove root ends of daikon seed sprouts and slice into thirds. Reconstitute dried *wakame* seaweed.

2. Boil soba noodles.

3. Rinse noodles well to remove all excess starch.

4. Chill in ice water.

5. Drain well and serve in dishes.

6. Top with wakame, *natto* and soft-boiled egg. Finish with soy sauce and remaining toppings and garnish with tempura crumbs.

Plain Udon

Sometimes just the noodles are enough

Plain noodles are served unadorned, without excessive ingredients.
My mother used to make plain udon noodles for me all the time, so this dish really takes me back.
Try it and you'll see that less can truly be more.

Ingredients (Serves 2)

2 servings udon noodles (frozen)
4 C Japanese soup broth (dashi. See below)
1 Tbsp each light soy sauce, mirin (sweet cooking
   wine)
Salt, to taste
Chopped spring onions (or scallions), for garnish

Instructions

1. Bring soup broth to a boil over low heat and
   add light soy sauce and mirin. Season with salt,
   adding gradually and checking until flavor is
   just right.
2. Boil udon noodles, drain well, and serve in
   bowls. Pour hot broth over noodles and top
   with chopped scallions.

How to Make Japanese Soup Broth (Dashi)
Add a handful of dried bonito flakes to 3 1/2 C of boiling water, simmer for 2 minutes, then scoop out bonito flakes. Feel free to substitute dried bonito flakes with other dried fish flakes that might be more common in your area.

Be Cautious With Your Salt

"Add salt gradually to taste." This is a pretty basic concept when cooking just about anything, but especially so with plain udon noodles. If you're not careful with your salt shaker, you could upset the balance and the simple appeal of the plain broth that makes or breaks this dish.
So please be cautious with your salt.

Pan-fried Chicken Soba

The crispy chicken adds a robust flavor

I love the combination of cold noodles and hot sauce. This recipe usually calls for duck, but I use chicken instead. I'm a big fan of the sweet and mellow flavor of chicken, and I love how the juices blend with the noodles for just the right degree of flavorful goodness.

Ingredients (Serves 2)

5 1/4 oz (150 g) soba noodles (dried)
1 chicken thigh
1 bunching onion (or leek)
1/2 Tbsp vegetable oil
3 C noodle dipping sauce (*men tsuyu*), diluted to taste
Grated wasabi, Japanese (*sansho*) pepper and roasted
  white sesame seeds, to taste

Instructions

1. Remove fat from chicken and cut into 2/5" (1 cm) strips. Chop bunching onion into 2/5" (1 cm) wide rounds.
2. Add oil to a heated pan and sauté chicken well on both sides. When chicken is cooked, add bunching onions and stir-fry.
3. When chicken and onions are lightly charred, pour in diluted noodle sauce. Bring to a boil, then reduce heat to low. Simmer for 5 minutes, occasionally removing surface foam.
4. Boil soba noodles, then rinse well. Chill in ice water and drain. Serve chilled noodles and chicken soup in separate dishes. Serve garnish ingredients on the side.

Fry chicken and bunching onion. They add a robust flavor to the broth.

Duck Noodle Soup with Parsley

Classy flavor is a piece of cake to make!

Duck has a strong and unique flavor, which Japanese parsley accentuates.

Ingredients (Serves 2)

7 oz (200 g) dried *kishimen* noodles (or udon noodles)
7 oz (200 g) duck breast
1/2 bundle Japanese parsley
1/2 Tbsp vegetable oil
4 C Japanese soup broth (see Reference Guide)
1 light Tbsp mirin (sweet cooking wine)
1/2 Tbsp soy sauce
Salt, to taste
Minced bunching onion (or leek) and pepper, to taste

Instructions

1. Cut duck into 1/5" (5 mm) thick slices. Cut Japanese parsley to 2" (5 cm) lengths.
2. Add oil to a heated soup pot and sauté duck. When meat is browned, add soup broth and bring to a boil over high heat. Reduce heat to low and simmer for 15 minutes, occasionally removing foam that floats to the surface.
3. Add mirin and soy sauce. Season gradually with salt, until flavor is just right. Add Japanese parsley and simmer briefly.
4. Cook *kishimen* noodles in boiling water, then rinse well. Drain noodles and add to hot soup. Serve in bowls and garnish with bunching onion and pepper.

Note
Parsley can be substituted with chrysanthemum or watercress.

Duck is chewy so slice thinly for easier eating.

Miso Simmered Udon

Flavorful red miso broth enriched with toasty sesame!

Blow off the steam as you slurp up the hot noodles, and the hearty root vegetables and rich hot broth will warm you up from the inside out. Firm frozen udon noodles are well suited to this simmered noodle soup.

Ingredients (Serves 2)

2 servings udon noodles (frozen)
5 1/4 oz (150 g) pork shoulder roast, thinly sliced
1 1/4" (3 cm) each daikon and carrot, peeled
3 taro roots (or sub parsnips or yams)
1 bunching onion (or green onion)
1 Tbsp sesame oil
3 C water

A ⌈ 1 1/2 Tbsp each red and white miso
  │ 1 Tbsp mirin
  │ 1/2 Tbsp soy sauce
  └ 2 Tbsp roasted white sesame seeds

Instructions

1. Cut pork into bite-size pieces. Thinly slice daikon then cut into quarters. Slice carrot then cut into half circles. Peel and quarter taro roots. Slice bunching onion diagonally to 1/5" (5 mm) widths.
2. Add oil to a heated soup pot and sauté pork over high heat. When pork is cooked add bunching onion and stir-fry until lightly browned. Add daikon, carrot, and taros. Stir-fry.
3. Stir-fry until all ingredients are well coated with oil and add water. Bring to a boil on high heat, then reduce heat to low. Simmer for 15 minutes. Add mixture A and stir. Boil udon noodles, drain, and add to soup and briefly simmer.

Nabeyaki Udon

It's fun to cook this popular dish yourself!

Udon noodles in broth, topped with special ingredients. Feel free to use store-bought tempura. The various toppings all add a dose of fun to this full-flavored dish. Personally, I like mine piping hot.

Ingredients (Serves 2)

2 servings udon noodles (frozen)
2 shrimp tempura (store-bought)
1/2 bundle spinach
2 slices fish cake (*kamaboko*.
   Or imitation crab legs)
Dried wheat gluten cakes (or *fu*)
2 eggs
3 C Japanese soup broth (see page 25)
1 Tbsp each light soy sauce, mirin
Salt, to taste
Seven-spice chili powder, to taste

Instructions

1. Blanch spinach, rinse well, and cut to 2" (5 cm) lengths. Soak wheat gluten cakes in water to reconstitute, then drain. Bring soup broth to a boil in a pot over low heat. Add light soy sauce and mirin. Season broth gradually with salt, checking repeatedly until flavor is just right.

2. Boil udon noodles, drain, and add to soup pot. Top with shrimp tempura, spinach, fish cakes and reconstituted wheat gluten cakes. Crack eggs into pot, cover and simmer over low heat for 2 minutes. Finish with seven-spice chili powder, if desired.

Miso-sautéed Udon with Pork

A full-bodied, rich dish!

Cold udon noodles, piping hot sauce. Sauce-soaked noodles retain their firm texture.
Sweet and robust sesame combines with the rich flavor of sautéed pork and bunching onion.
Chilled udon noodles wrapped in this miso sauce creates a sublime taste experience.

Ingredients (Serves 2)

2 servings udon noodles (frozen)
5 1/4 oz (150 g) pork belly, thinly sliced
2 bunching onions (or green onions)
1 Tbsp sesame oil

A ⎡ 2 Tbsp sake
⎢ 1 1/2 Tbsp red miso
⎢ 1 Tbsp mirin (sweet cooking wine)
⎢ 1/2 Tbsp sugar
⎣ 2 to 3 Tbsp ground black sesame seeds

1 nub ginger, grated
Grated garlic, to taste
Sesame oil, to taste

Instructions

1. Cut pork into bite-size pieces. Thinly slice bunching onion on the bias. Combine mixture A.
2. Add sesame oil to a heated pan and sauté pork and bunching onion over high heat. When well browned, add mixture A and coat.
3. Boil udon noodles, rinse, and chill in ice water. Drain and place in a bowl. Add grated ginger, garlic, and sauce and pork from step 2. Coat noodles well. Finish with sesame oil, if desired.

Coat noodles with sauce.

Sesame oil adds a nice fragrance. Add as much as you like.

Yakisoba

I always thought yakisoba can be made in a flash, nothing fancy, no difficult tricks to remember.
Unfortunately, it's actually a little harder than I would like to admit to cook yakisoba just right.
If you're using a Teflon-coated pan, there's little worry of the noodles getting
hopelessly stuck to the surface, so you can focus on stirring quickly and energetically,
coating the noodles with oil and finishing the dish with flair.
If you're using a regular pan, start by heating it well before adding anything.
Then coat the pan with oil thoroughly, and the pan is ready to go.
Stir-fry the ingredients with gusto. Don't feel like you have to rush, though.
Try to keep a relaxed mood as you whip the ingredients across the pan.
If the noodles stick a bit, you can always say
that you *meant* to have that crunchy, lightly charred flavor.

5. Stir-fry w[...]
sprouts ar[...]
through. A[...]
noodles.

Yakisoba with Ham

Pack a punch with a trilogy of tongue-tingling flavors!

Onion + ginger + garlic = delicious. These three are the key to the simple and unassuming appeal of this dish.
Allow noodles to cook undisturbed a bit before you start stir-frying. When noodles are tender enough to pull apart, stir-fry well. This is the trick to cooking delicious yakisoba.

Yakisoba with Five Point Sauce

Charred, crispy and crunchy

Spread noodles out in a pan, then just let them sit and fry. No soup broth needed. The meat, seafood, and vegetables add more than enough savory flavors to this dish.

Ingredients (Serves 2)

2 servings yakisoba (steamed ramen) noodles
1/2 Tbsp vegetable oil
2 Tbsp sake
1 1/2 Tbsp sesame oil

Five Point Sauce

3 1/2 oz (100 g) pork shoulder, thinly sliced
3 oz (80 g) frozen cuttlefish (or squid)
1/3 bundle *komatsuna* (or mustard greens or spinach)
1 1/4" (3 cm) carrot
5 boiled quail eggs
1 clove garlic, minced
1 nub ginger, minced
1 Tbsp sesame oil
Salt, to taste
2 Tbsp sake
1 Tbsp each oyster sauce, soy sauce
1 1/4 C water
A ⎡ 2 light Tbsp potato (or corn) starch
  ⎣ 3 Tbsp water
Japanese mustard paste, to taste

1 Fry Noodles

1. Add oil to a heated pan, then add yaki-soba noodles. Pour on sake and pull noodles apart.

2. Spread loosened noodles over pan surface and add sesame oil.

3. Let noodles fry slowly, undisturbed, over medium heat.

4. Fry until the bottom of the noodles are a delicious golden brown, then turn over. Repeat on opposite side. Divide fried noodles in half and serve on plates.

2 Make Sauce

5. Cut pork into bite-size pieces. Thaw cuttlefish and pat dry, cut in half lengthwise and then into 2/5" (1 cm) wide strips. Cut komatsuna to 2" (5 cm) lengths. Slice carrot into thin half-circles. Combine mixture A.

6. Add sesame oil to a heated pan. Sauté garlic and ginger on low heat until fragrant. Add pork and stir-fry over high heat.

7. When pork is browned add cuttlefish and stir-fry.

8. When cuttlefish is coated with oil, add carrot slices and stir-fry until cooked. Add komatsuna and add a dash of salt. Stir-fry until tender.

9. Add boiled quail eggs and stir. Add sake, oyster sauce, soy sauce, and water.

10. Bring to a boil, then turn off heat. Stir mixture A well just before adding, and stir into sauce. Turn on heat and simmer until sauce thickens.

11. Top yakisoba with sauce and serve mustard paste on the side.

Yakisoba with Raw Egg + Yakisoba Omelet

Upgraded versions of two popular Japanese dishes!

Sauce-smothered yakisoba are very popular in Japan.
My version includes generous helpings of vegetables, shrimp and sausage.
Adding ketchup to the sauce is another trick I recommend.
If you fold it all up into an omelet, kids will love it. Heck, even the grown-ups will be thrilled.

Ingredients (Serves 2)

2 servings yakisoba (steamed ramen) noodles
3 1/2 oz (100 g) pork shoulder, thinly sliced
1/8 head cabbage
2 to 3 small sausages
1 Tbsp vegetable oil
1/4 C water
3 Tbsp *chuno* sauce
 (or Tonkatsu or Worcestershire sauce)
1/2 Tbsp ketchup

2 Tbsp ground white sesame seeds
2 Tbsp *sakura* (dwarf) shrimp
 (or salad shrimp)
2 to 3 Tbsp tempura crumbs (*tenkasu*)
1 Tbsp pickled red ginger, minced
Aonori dried seaweed, to taste
- **For raw egg sauce, use 2 eggs**
- **For omelet, use 2 eggs, 2 pinches sugar,
  1 pinch salt, 1 Tbsp vegetable oil,
  dash each ketchup and mayonnaise**

Instructions

1. Cut pork and cabbage into bite-size pieces. Cut sausage on the bias into 1/5" (5 mm) thick slices.
2. Add vegetable oil to a heated pan and stir-fry pork over high heat. When pork is lightly browned add sausage and stir-fry. Add cabbage and continue stir-frying.
3. Add yakisoba noodles and pour in water. When noodles are tender enough, pull apart and stir. Add *chuno* sauce and ketchup and stir to coat. Stir in ground sesame seeds, *sakura* shrimp, tempura crumbs, pickled ginger, and seaweed.
4. Dip noodles in raw eggs as you eat, or cook eggs to make yakisoba omelets. For omelet version: Transfer noodles to a dish and wash frying pan. Add salt and sugar to eggs and blend well. Return pan to heat and add oil. Pour in eggs and cook until half-done. Return noodles to pan and fold sides of omelet over noodles. Cover pan with a dish and flip over, transferring omelet from the pan to the dish. You can adjust the shape of the omelet with a paper towel. Top with ketchup and mayonnaise.

For the yakisoba omelet, you can make one serving and split it in half, or you can make each separately.

Crunchy Yakisoba
(Thin and Thick Noodles)
Chicken-based salty sauce is the secret!

Just top deep-fried yakisoba noodles with thick sauce.
Fresh chicken broth is the secret of the sauce.
It's easy, though. Just put the chicken in water and boil.
Oyster sauce adds another dimension.

Ingredients (Serves 2)

2 servings crispy yakisoba or
  chow mein (thick or thin styles)
5 1/4 oz (150 g) chicken breast
4 shrimp
1/8 head Napa cabbage
1/2 bundle garlic chives
1 clove garlic
1 nub ginger
A ⌈2 Tbsp potato (or corn)
  │   starch
  └3 Tbsp water

1 Tbsp sesame oil
2 Tbsp sake
2 C water
1/2 Tbsp oyster sauce
Salt, to taste
Sesame oil, rice vinegar and
  Japanese mustard paste, to
  taste

Instructions

1. Cut chicken into bite-size
   pieces. Shell shrimp and slice
   open along back. Devein. Divide Napa cabbage into stems
   and leaves. Chop leaves into
   bite-size pieces and julienne
   stems. Cut chives to 2" (5
   cm) lengths. Mince garlic and
   ginger. Combine mixture A.
2. Add sesame oil to a heated
   pan and sauté chicken, garlic,
   and ginger over medium-high
   heat until chicken is browned.
   Add sake and stir. Add water
   and oyster sauce. Bring to
   a boil over high heat, then
   reduce heat to low. Simmer for
   5 minutes.
3. Add shrimp and simmer
   until cooked. Add cabbage
   and simmer briefly. Season
   gradually with salt. Add
   chives, quickly stir, and turn
   off heat. Stir mixture A and
   mix into sauce. Turn on heat
   and simmer until sauce
   thickens.
4. Serve fried yakisoba in
   dishes and top with sauce.
   Top with extra sesame oil,
   and rice vinegar. Serve mustard paste on the side.

Rice Vermicelli

Rice vermicelli is popular in Asia.
They tend to stick together easily when fried so you have to use plenty of oil, turn the heat to high, and cook them quickly.
Once the noodles are coated with hot oil, you don't have to worry about them clumping together.
Focus on cooking so quickly that the noodles don't have a chance to stick. But if you find yourself in a sticky situation, just add a little oil and dig in with a pair of chopsticks and loosen the noodles up.
Just ignore any little bits of noodle left clinging to the pan. You might think that's a bit sloppy, but don't worry, that's the best way to cook 'em.
Making soup with rice vermicelli, on the other hand, is a whole different story.
You can't go wrong no matter what you do.

Fried Rice Vermicelli

Be generous with the sesame oil!

When making fried rice vermicelli it's important to keep checking on the status of the noodles and your pan.

Keep adding sesame oil to keep everything in good order.

Also, don't fuss with the noodles once they're in the pan. Fry 'em up and get 'em out.

Ingredients (Serves 2)
3 oz (80 g) clear rice noodles
3 1/2 oz (100 g) ground meat
1/2 bunch garlic chives
1/2 bag bean sprouts
1 clove garlic
1 nub ginger
2 eggs
3 Tbsp *sakura* (dwarf) shrimp
  (or salad shrimp)
1 1/2 to 2 Tbsp sesame oil
2 Tbsp sake
1 Tbsp oyster sauce
Salt and pepper, to taste

Instructions
1. Soak rice vermicelli in water according to package directions. Cut chives to 2" (5 cm) lengths. Remove root ends of bean sprouts. Mince garlic and ginger. Lightly beat eggs just enough to combine whites and yolks.
2. Add sesame oil to a heated pan and sauté garlic and ginger over low heat until fragrant. Add ground meat and stir-fry over high heat. When meat is lightly browned add bean sprouts and stir-fry until cooked through. Add *sakura* shrimp and chives. Stir thoroughly.
3. Drain vermicelli. Move stir-fried ingredients to one side of the pan and pour in eggs. When eggs are cooked, add vermicelli. Stir-fry, mixing noodles and other ingredients together. When vermicelli are cooked through add sake and oyster sauce. Season with salt and pepper to taste.

Pho

Pho are Vietnamese rice noodles.
They are thin, flat and cook fast.
Just add softened noodles to hot soup and they're good to go.
There's no need to consider cooking time to preserve
firmness or texture with pho noodles.
If they're tender enough to be pulled apart, they're ready.
Even if they get a little overdone from sitting
in the soup too long, no problem.
They taste good that way, too.

Vietnamese Chicken Noodle Soup

Chicken soup with a hint of lime steals the scene!

This dish is called *Pho Ga* in Vietnamese. There is nothing complicated about it.
Just toss chicken and some spices in a pot and simmer. Finish with a squeeze of lime.
Simple. And the satisfaction of homemade soup can't be beat.

Ingredients (Serves 2)

3 oz (80 g) Vietnamese rice noodles (pho)
4 boneless chicken wings
4 1/4 C (1 liter) water
1 clove garlic
1 nub ginger
A
  - 5 to 6 stems lemongrass
  - 5 to 6 dried Kieffer lime leaves
  - 2 slices galangal root
3 leaves lettuce
1/2 small tomato
1/4 bag bean sprouts
Juice of 1/2 lime
1 1/2 Tbsp Nam pla (Thai fish sauce)
Salt, cilantro and pepper, to taste

Instructions

1. Place water, chicken wings, garlic, ginger, and mixture A in a pan and bring to a boil over high heat. Reduce heat to low and simmer 30 minutes, occasionally removing foam that floats to the surface.
2. Shred lettuce into bite-size pieces. Cut tomato into small wedges. Remove root ends of bean sprouts. Soak pho noodles according to package directions.
3. When soup has simmered for 30 minutes, stir in Nam pla and lime juice. Season with salt gradually to taste. Add bean sprouts and lettuce. Add softened noodles and gently pull apart. Simmer briefly. Serve in dishes and garnish with tomato and cilantro. Finish with pepper.

Note
See page 15 for info about dried Kieffer lime leaves and galangal root.

Naengmyeon

This Korean noodle dish is very popular in Japan.
It's all because of those deliciously sticky and super chewy
naengmyeon noodles. You can cook noodles according to your own
preference, but they're best when cooked until al dente.
In Korea, the broth is usually made from beef, but light chicken
broth is tasty, too. Well-pickled and deliciously spiced kimchi is
a perfect accent for this dish. The sweet flavor of apple and
Japanese pear are delightful complements.

Naengmyeon in Chicken Broth

The chicken makes the soup

In Korea they use beef broth for this dish.
But I like to use the healthier option of chicken.
The delicious flavor of chilled, clear, gelatinous soup is
wonderful, and holds up against the firm Korean noodles.

Ingredients (Serves 2)

2 servings naengmyeon (or reimen) noodles
2 boneless chicken thighs
A ⌈ 1 bunching onion (or green onion) (green leaves)
⌊ 1 clove garlic, halved
⌊ 1 nub ginger, cut in thirds
4 1/4 C (1 liter) water
1/2 cucumber
1 boiled egg
Apple, julienned, to taste
Kimchi and roasted white sesame seeds, for garnish
Salt and rice vinegar, to taste

Instructions

1. Remove fat from chicken and cut into 2/5" (1 cm)
   wide strips. Bring water to a boil in a soup pot and
   add mixture A and chicken. Simmer over low heat for
   1 hour, occasionally removing surface foam. After 1
   hour, season with salt, adding gradually until flavor
   is on the strong side. Remove A ingredients and set
   chicken aside. When soup has cooled off, place in
   refrigerator to chill.
2. Slice cucumber in half lengthwise then diagonally
   into thin slices. Halve boiled egg.
3. Cook noodles in boiling water and rinse. Chill in ice
   water and drain well. Serve noodles in bowls and top
   with chilled soup. Add chicken, cucumber, boiled
   egg, apple and kimchi. Sprinkle with roasted sesame
   seeds and add rice vinegar, if desired.

The Ultimate Noodle Experience

Simmer slowly, fry 'til good and crispy... For the ultimate noodle experience, it's worth it.

Cha Shao

Cut meat into thick slices and savor the simmered flavor!

Ingredients (Serves 4)

21 oz (600 g) pork shoulder

A ⌈ 1 bunching onion (or green onion) (green leaves)
  | 1 clove garlic, halved
  ⌊ 1 nub ginger, halved

B ⌈ 2/5 C sake
  | 2 Tbsp soy sauce
  | 1 Tbsp each oyster sauce and sugar
  ⌊ 1 tsp sesame oil

Note
Add extra water as needed to keep pork covered.

1. In a large soup pot, bring water (about 5 C) to a boil. Add pork and mixture A and bring to a boil again. Reduce heat to low and simmer for 90 minutes, occasionally removing surface foam.

2. Poke meat with a skewer. If it goes in easily and comes out cleanly, the pork is ready.

3. Remove pork and A ingredients and reserve broth.

Cha Shao Ramen

Since this recipe uses homemade simmered pork, you can add as many slices of meat cut as thickly as your heart desires.
If you use leftover broth for the noodle soup then nothing is wasted. This is the perfect noodle dish for meat lovers.

Ingredients (Serves 2)

2 servings Chinese (ramen) noodles
Cha shao, to taste
Soup
⌐4 C broth from page 46
 1 1/2 to 2 Tbsp soy sauce
 1 Tbsp sake
 Pinch sugar
└Salt, to taste
1/2 bundle spinach, blanched
1 boiled egg
menma (dried bamboo shoots) and
   pepper, to taste

Instructions

1. Heat broth over medium heat until warm. Add soy sauce, sake, and sugar. Stir. Add salt to taste.
2. Cut spinach to 2" (5 cm) lengths. Slice boiled egg in half. Cut *cha shao* into slices of desired thickness.
3. Boil noodles.
4. Serve piping hot soup in a large bowl. Drain noodles well and add to soup. Top with *cha shao* slices, spinach, boiled egg and *menma*. Sprinkle with pepper.

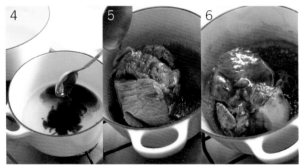

4. Bring mixture B to boil in a soup pot.

5. Add pork from step 3 and simmer over medium heat, occasionally turning meat over, coating with sauce.

6. Simmer until liquid is reduced to amount shown in above picture.

Fried Mochi

Ingredients (Serves 2)
2 slices mochi
(glutinous rice cakes)
Oil, for deep frying

Fried Mochi

Use high heat and fry quickly!

1. Halve mochi.

2. In a pan, heat about 4/5" (2 cm) oil until bubbles appear when chopsticks are inserted (appx. 375°F (200°C)).

3. Add mochi to oil and fry until golden brown, occasionally turning over. If you fry too slowly, the insides will leak out, so be careful.

Udon with Fried Mochi

Mochi and udon noodles are two peas in a pod when it comes to chewy texture. The toasty sweet flavor of fried mochi is a mouth-watering match for udon noodles. The richness of the oil-infused broth creates an excellent base.

Ingredients (Serves 2)
2 servings udon noodles (frozen)
4 fried mochi (see above)
Soup
  3 1/4 C Japanese soup broth
    (see reference guide)
  1 Tbsp light soy sauce
  1 Tbsp mirin
    (sweet cooking wine)
  Salt, to taste
2 slices grilled fish cake
  (*kamaboko*. or sub. imitation
  crab sticks)
Chopped scallions, for garnish
Seven spice powder, to taste

Instructions
1. Bring soup broth to a boil on low heat. Add soy sauce and mirin. Season with salt, adding gradually until flavor is just right.
2. Boil udon noodles and serve in bowls. Pour hot soup from step 1 over noodles and top with fried mochi, grilled fish cake and scallions. Finish with seven spice chili powder, if desired.

Making Shrimp Tempura

Ingredients (Serves 2)

6 shrimp

Batter
- 3/4 C flour
- 1/3 C water
- 1 egg
- Ice

Flour, for coating

Oil for deep frying

1. Shell and devein shrimp. Cut off tail tips and scrape off dirt and liquid with a knife.

2. Make several slits along the belly of shrimp and bend backward until they snap straight.

3. Combine batter ingredients.

4. In a pan, heat 1 1/4" (3 cm) oil to medium high (345°F (160°C)). Coat shrimp in flour, dip in batter, and slide into hot oil.

5. For added volume, drop extra batter onto shrimp with cooking chopsticks.

6. Fry until coating is crispy, occasionally turning over.

Shrimp Tempura

Big, fluffy and crispy crunchy!

Shrimp Tempura Soba

Devour the freshly fried tempura quickly, while they're still crispy. Or, savor soft tempura soaked in soup broth as it melts off the shrimp. Both are truly delicious and delightful ways of enjoying this recipe. Which is why you need three shrimp tempura. Just two won't do.

Ingredients (Serves 2)

5 1/4 oz (150 g) soba noodles

6 shrimp tempura (see above)

1/2 bunch spinach

Soup
- 3 1/4 C Japanese soup broth (see reference guide)
- 1 Tbsp light soy sauce
- 1 Tbsp mirin (sweet cooking wine)
- Salt, to taste

Yuzu peel (or lemon zest), to taste

Instructions

1. Blanch spinach and rinse well. Drain and cut to 2" (5 cm) lengths.

2. Bring broth to a boil over low heat and add soy sauce and mirin. Season with salt, adding gradually.

3. Boil soba noodles and rinse well. Blanch noodles to reheat, then serve in bowls. Pour hot soup from step 2 over noodles. Top with shrimp tempura, spinach, and *yuzu* peel.

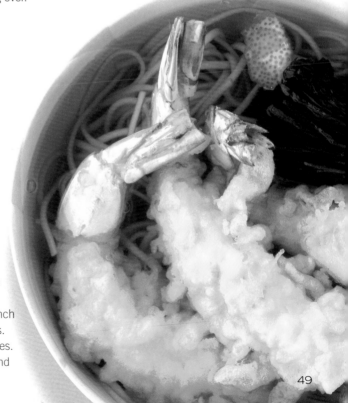

Homemade Udon

Full of flavor with a rich, dense texture!

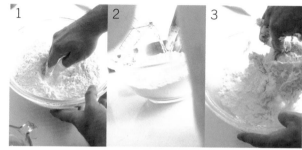

1. Combine pastry flour and bread flour. Add about 2/3 C lukewarm water and stir by hand.

2. Slowly add another 1/3 C water, a little at a time. Add as much water as the dough can hold.

3. Mix well by hand until dough can be formed into a large ball.

4. Dust cutting board with flour. Knead dough. Put power into it and knead until dough is soft and smooth.

5. Wrap dough in plastic film and let sit at room temperature for 5 minutes.

6. After 5 minutes, divide dough in half. Dust cutting board with flour and roll out one half of dough to a thickness of about 1/8" (3 mm).

7. This is the thickness to aim for, but slightly thicker noodles are tasty, too.

8. Dust dough well with flour and fold into thirds. Cut into 1/4 to 1/3" (5 to 7 mm) wide strips. Repeat with other half of dough.

9. Dust noodles with flour to prevent them from sticking together.

Ultimate Homemade Udon Noodles

Homemade noodles take time and energy to make, which is why it's best to savor them with minimal dressing. Nothing fancy; just sprinkle with soy sauce. So simple, but truly luxurious. It doesn't matter if the noodles aren't all the same thickness. That's part of what makes them so good.

Ingredients (Serves 4)

Udon noodles
- 3 1/2 C bread flour
- 1/2 C pastry flour
- 1 1/4 to 1 1/2 C lukewarm water

Flour, for dusting
4 egg yolks
Ginger, grated
Chopped scallions, roasted white
   sesame seeds and soy sauce, to taste

Note
- When rolling out dough, it's important to roll right past the edges. The shape is unimportant.
- If you want to eat your udon hot, you can enjoy it straight out of the pot. You can also reheat them by blanching before adding the toppings.

10. Boil noodles.

11. Cook for 5 to 7 minutes, occasionally stirring.

12. Rinse noodles well.

13. Chill well in ice water, then drain. Serve in bowls. Top with egg yolk and other condiments. Finish with soy sauce and roasted sesame seeds.

Potato Gnocchi

Knead well for a chewy, rich texture!

1. Peel and quarter potatoes. Soak in water for 3 minutes.

2. In a pan, cover potatoes with water and bring to a boil. Cook until a skewer can be easily inserted. Drain, then cook potatoes over high heat to evaporate excess water.

3. Add egg, salt and grated parmesan cheese to potatoes. Use a masher (or fork) and mash ingredients together until well blended.

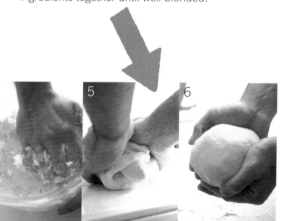

Potato Gnocchi with Gorgonzola Sauce

The strong and unique flavor of Gorgonzola turns mild with the addition of fresh cream. But you can always substitute cream cheese instead if you're not a fan of strongly flavored cheese. Let the dough sit while you make the sauce, and you'll get deliciously smooth gnocchi.

Ingredients (Serves 4)
Gnocchi
- 2 potatoes (appx. 12 oz total)
- 1 egg
- 1/2 tsp salt
- 4 Tbsp grated Parmesan cheese
- 1 1/3 to 1 2/3 cups pastry flour
- Flour, for dusting

Sauce
- 3 oz (80 g) Gorgonzola cheese
- 1 clove garlic, minced
- 1 Tbsp olive oil
- 1 Tbsp white wine
- 4/5 C fresh cream
- 2/5 C milk

Salt, pepper, olive oil and roasted walnuts, to taste

4. Add 1 C pastry flour and mix in by hand. Add remaining 1/3 to 2/3 C flour gradually, kneading repeatedly until flour is absorbed and dough is no longer sticky.

5. Move dough to a cutting board or work surface and continue kneading. The firmness should be slightly tougher than an ear lobe.

6. When dough is soft and smooth, wrap in plastic film and let sit for 10 minutes.

12. Boil gnocchi in lightly salted water for 5 to 6 minutes. Try one, and if there's no dry, pasty flavor it's done. Drain in a colander.

13. Add gnocchi to sauce from step 9 and mix, cooking over high heat. Stir to coat. Add salt as needed. Serve in dishes and sprinkle olive oil, pepper, and roasted walnuts.

10. Dust cutting board or working surface with flour and break up gnocchi dough into approximately 3/4" (2 cm) diameter chunks. Roll into balls.

11. Press thumb into center of each ball to create an impression.

7. While dough is resting, make sauce. Add olive oil to a heated pan and sauté minced garlic on low heat.

8. When garlic is lightly browned, raise heat to medium and add white wine. Briefly stir-fry. Add fresh cream and milk.

9. Add Gorgonzola cheese to sauce in small clumps. Crush cheese with a spoon as it melts. Season with salt and pepper.

Dumpling Soup

Roll the dough around.
That's all the kneading you need!

1. Cut daikon into 1/5" (5 mm) thick quarter-circle slices and carrot into 1/5" (5 mm) thick half moon slices. Chop scallions to 2" (5 cm) lengths. Scrub burdock with a rough brush to remove dirt and peel skin. Shave burdock into very thin slices and soak in water. Cut *konnyaku* into bite-size pieces cook briefly in boiling water. Cut fried tofu (*aburaage*) in half lengthwise and slice each half into 2/5" (1 cm) wide strips. Cut pork into bite-size pieces.

2. Add sesame oil to a heated pan and sauté pork over high heat. When meat is lightly browned add vegetables, fried tofu, and *konnyaku*. Stir-fry.

3. When all ingredients are coated with oil, pour in soup stock. Bring to a boil over high heat. Reduce heat to low and simmer for 15 to 20 minutes. Remove surface foam as necessary.

4. When daikon is tender add soy sauce and mirin. Stir. Season with salt to taste.

5. Make dumplings. Mix flour and water thoroughly.

6. Keep kneading dough. Don't worry if it sticks to your hands.

Hearty Soup with Dumplings

Plop those dumplings one by one into the pot. This healthy and filling soup chock full of delicious vegetables will warm your heart and fill your stomach.

Ingredients (Serves 4)

Soup dumplings
- 1 2/3 C flour
- 2/3 C water

1" (3 cm) daikon
2" (5 cm) carrot
1/2 bundle scallions
1/2 burdock root
1/2 block *konnyaku* (konjac jelly)
1 pouch *aburaage* (thin fried tofu)
7 oz (200 g) pork shoulder, thinly sliced
1 to 2 Tbsp sesame oil
6 C Japanese soup broth (see Reference Guide)
3 Tbsp soy sauce
1 1/2 to 2 Tbsp mirin (sweet cooking wine)
Salt, to taste
3 Tbsp ground white sesame seeds

7. When dough is smooth and no longer sticky, break into bite-size chunks by hand.

8. Drop dumplings into soup pot, add scallions, and simmer for 3-5 minutes. Serve in bowls and sprinkle with ground sesame seeds.

The Noodles You Will Find In This Book

Chinese noodles

Chinese noodles (fresh)

Chinese noodles (dried)

Cook simply, with good intentions

The world is full of all kinds of noodles. The word "pasta," for example, encompasses all kinds of noodles. Japanese soba and udon noodles, too, come in a wide variety, from thick to thin, smooth to coarse. They're all called "udon" or "soba," but each variety has its own unique flavor and texture. All noodles have their own historical background, as well as a fail-safe recipe or two. That's why it's important to pay proper respect to the individuality of each type of noodle. There's no need to get fancy or do anything extreme. Even pasta designed for use in cold dishes is a relatively new invention. Technically, new and unusual recipes could easily become standard. However, I prefer to not add any extreme changes or really crazy ideas. I just tweak traditional ingredient combinations slightly, or come up with a minor twist on basic seasonings and sauces. For example, using the water leftover from boiling pasta in the sauce is a very simple technique, but not something many people would come up with. In short, when cooking noodles, pay proper respect to cooks that blazed the trail for you, and avoid overly ambitious flavorings and kooky combinations. Approach your noodles with a humble heart on your sleeve.

Japanese noodles

Frozen, fresh, dried—pick whichever you like. Just remember when using dried noodles rinse well after boiling to get rid of excess starch.

Udon (dried)

Kishimen (flat udon) (dried)

Soba (dried)

Udon (frozen)

Udon (fresh)

Soba (fresh)

Yakisoba

Steamed yakisoba

Fried yakisoba (thin)

Fried yakisoba (thick)

56

Asian Noodles

Rice vermicelli (thick)

Rice vermicelli (thin)

Pho noodles

Naengmyeon

Naengmyeon

Thin Japanese Noodles

Oil is often used in creating extra-thin somen noodles, so it's best to let them sit before use. Rinse well after boiling.

Somen (fine white noodles)

Hiyamugi (thicker than somen, thinner than udon)

Pasta

Spaghetti noodles are usually somewhere around 1/15" (1.7 mm) thick. Thinner noodles are called fedelini, and spaghettini is between spaghetti and fedelini in size. Capellini and vermicelli are even thinner pasta noodles. Fettuccini and tagliatelle are flat pasta noodles. Linguine is flat spaghetti with rounded-edges.

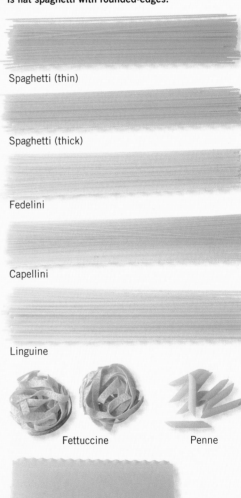

Spaghetti (thin)

Spaghetti (thick)

Fedelini

Capellini

Linguine

Fettuccine

Penne

Lasagna

Pasta

The word "pasta" refers to the wide world of Italian noodles.
As reflected in the words "al dente," you'll want to be careful about how long you cook your pasta.
Specific cooking times will depend on how you plan to prepare the noodles,
but as a general rule cook for one minute less than the time indicated by the package directions.
Pasta continues cooking when added to boiling sauce, and
even after transferring them to a colander the steam keeps heating them.
So noodles that initially seem slightly undercooked end up just right.
But always do a taste test, just to be sure.
In my experience, some noodles are still too firm to eat even when cooked exactly as directed.
For chilled pasta dishes, keep in mind that noodles
firm up when placed in ice water, so boil them a little longer than the time indicated.
Salt added to boiling water plays two important roles:
it not only raises the boiling point, but also seasons the pasta.
Thick, creamy sauces that coat noodles well don't really need extra salt,
but chilled pasta doesn't always absorb flavor very well. So use a decent dose of salt.

Vongole Bianco

Al dente noodles with a fresh scent of the sea!

This is quite possibly my favorite pasta dish.
Plenty of garlic gives it a rich aroma.
Add littleneck clams, stir-fry, pour in the boiling liquid.
Simple yet irresistibly delicious.
This recipe is a staple in my diet.

Vongole Bianco

Ingredients (Serves 2)
6 oz (160 g) fedelini
10 1/2 oz (300 g) littleneck clams,
    soaked in water to remove sand
3 cloves garlic, minced
2 Tbsp olive oil
10 *shiso* leaves (or basil or mint)
Salt and pepper, to taste

1. Chop *shiso* leaves. Rub clam shells together to remove dirt, then rinse thoroughly.

2. Add plenty of salt to a pot full of boiling water.

3. Add pasta. Set timer for 1 minute less than time indicated by package directions.

4. Stir occasionally.

5. Add olive oil to a heated pan and sauté garlic over low heat.

Note
Garlic cloves sometimes have green cores. These burn easily and can turn bitter, so if there's a core, remove it before mincing.

6. When garlic is lightly browned add clams. Stir-fry over high heat.

7. When clams open add a half ladleful of pasta boiling liquid.

8. When timer goes off, drain pasta and add to sauce in pan.

9. Stir quickly. Clams and pasta broth are both salty, so be sure to check the flavor before adding any salt.

10. Sprinkle chopped *shiso*. Stir, serve, and finish with pepper.

Linguine in Seafood Sauce

Sauce steeped in the rich flavor of marine bounty!

For this recipe, don't worry about maintaining the textures of
the shrimp and squid. Just simmer them thoroughly.
You will be amazed at how much flavor they add to the sauce.
Soft simmered seafood blends in well with pasta for
a delicious dish. Use toothsome linguine noodles.

Fettucine with Mushroom Sauce

Knock them out with a garlic punch!

It's important to bring out the aroma of the mushrooms with a dose of garlic, so sauté slowly to get that robust flavor. Take your time. Wide, flat pasta coated in creamy sauce. Delicious.

Carbonara

Be generous with the pepper and garlic!

The right balance of saltiness is always important,
but especially with carbonara.
If it's not salty enough you'll get bored with the weak flavor.
But too much salt is an even bigger problem, so be cautious.
Taste as you cook, and if it seems too weak don't hesitate to
add extra salt.

Spaghetti with Egg and Ricotta Tomato Sauce

Tangy sauce with creamy egg and cheese!

Let me level with you: this recipe is not mine.
I respectfully stole it from my friend after eating this
scrumptious pasta dish topped with ricotta cheese at his
restaurant. The ingredients and sauce are slightly different, but the genius stroke of adding mild ricotta cheese
is not my idea. So if you like this recipe, tell people that
"the recipe Kentaro stole from Taku" is delicious.

Beef and Spinach Linguine

Tangy and slightly spicy sauce tingles your taste buds!

Refreshing spinach and beef make a great combination,
and the dense flavor of sun-dried tomatoes serves to further
accentuate the beef. Use leftover boiling liquid for
a sturdy yet mellow sauce. Pasta broth is amazing stuff.

Napolitan Egg Spaghetti

Pasta with a Japanese twist

Don't use al dente pasta for Napolitan Spaghetti. This dish is best with noodles that have been left to stew awhile.
For the sauce, use ketchup only. No need to get picky or use any tricks.
Finish with fluffy egg sauce for a surprisingly simple yet sublime combination.

Spaghetti with Egg and Ricotta Tomato Sauce

Ingredients (Serves 2)
6 oz (160 g) spaghetti
Ricotta cheese, to taste
2 soft-boiled eggs
3 small sausages
2 cloves garlic
2 red chili peppers
1 1/2 Tbsp olive oil
14 oz (400 g) canned whole tomatoes
6 fresh basil leaves
Olive oil, salt and pepper, to taste

Instructions
1. Cut sausage in half lengthwise then into 1/8" (3 mm) slices. Mince garlic. Remove stems and seeds of chili peppers. Cut up whole tomatoes in the can, using scissors.
2. Add olive oil to a heated pan and sauté garlic over low heat until lightly browned. Add sausage and chili peppers and stir-fry over high heat. When sausage is browned, add tomatoes and simmer over medium heat for 5 minutes. Season to taste with salt.
3. Boil pasta in salted water for 1 minute less than time indicated by package directions. Drain pasta and add to sauce in pan. Add basil and stir. Serve in dishes and top with soft-boiled egg and ricotta cheese. Finish with olive oil and pepper.

Note
Ricotta is a creamy Italian "whey cheese" made from fresh whey. It has a light, refreshing flavor with no edge to it. Mozzarella cheese also works well in this recipe.

Beef and Spinach Linguine

Ingredients (Serves 2)
6 oz (160 g) linguine
1 bundle fresh spinach
5 1/4 oz (150 g) beef shoulder roast, thinly sliced
3 cloves garlic
1 to 2 red chili peppers
3 dried tomatoes
1 1/2 Tbsp olive oil
Salt and pepper, to taste

Instructions
1. Cut beef into bite-size pieces. Crush garlic. Shred chili peppers and deseed. Reconstitute sun-dried tomatoes in lukewarm water, squeeze out water, and cut in half.
2. Add olive oil to a heated pan and sauté garlic and chili peppers over low heat until garlic is lightly browned. Add beef and stir-fry over high heat. Start boiling pasta in salted water.
3. When beef is browned add reconstituted tomatoes and 1 1/2 ladlefuls of pasta boiling liquid. Stir-fry.
4. Cook pasta 1 minute less than time indicated by package directions, drain well, and add to sauce in pan. Season to taste with salt and pepper. Add spinach and mix until wilted.

Napolitan Egg Spaghetti

Ingredients (Serves 2)
6 oz (160 g) spaghetti
4 slices ham
1 green pepper
1/2 onion
1 3/4 oz (45 g) sliced mushrooms, canned
2 eggs
1 1/2 Tbsp vegetable oil
4 Tbsp ketchup
Grated parmesan cheese, to taste
Salt and pepper, to taste

Note
**Stir well after adding ketchup
for a mild flavor.**

1 Prepare Pasta

1. Boil pasta in salted water for 30 seconds longer than time indicated by package directions.

2. Drain pasta and coat with 1/2 Tbsp oil. Set aside.

2 Make Toppings

3. Cut ham into 1/2" (1 1/2 cm) strips, julienne green pepper lengthwise, and slice onion along the grain. Drain canned mushrooms. Lightly beat eggs just enough to blend whites and yolks.

4. Add 1 Tbsp oil to a heated pan and sauté onions over medium heat until translucent.

5. Add ham, green pepper, and mushrooms. Stir-fry over high heat.

6. When ingredients are lightly browned add spaghetti. Stir in well.

7. Add ketchup. Stir to coat.

8. Add grated parmesan cheese and season to taste with salt and pepper.

9. Pour in eggs along edge of pan and cook slowly over medium heat. Don't stir until eggs are done.

Fedelini with
Crab and Cabbage

Unbelievably easy, indescribably delicious!

The mild flavor of crab is a perfect match for the sweetness of cabbage.
Just shred cabbage by hand and add it to the pasta pot a minute or
two before the noodles are ready to go.
And for the crab, just used canned meat. Super simple.
Thin fedelini is well-suited to the mild flavor of this dish.

Spaghetti with
Potato and Basil

**Potato and pine nuts add a
savory fragrance!**

No meat, but plenty rich. Garlic and
potatoes are the key, and the addition
of pasta boiling liquid is also not to
be overlooked. Simple pasta dishes like
this rely on getting the amount of salt
just right. Be careful not to add
too much, though. Extra salt can
always be added later at the table.

Capellini with Eggplant and Anchovies

Light and refreshing with a squeeze of lemon!

Tasty summer vegetables complement well-chilled angel hair pasta. Add a squeeze of lemon to the dressing for an invigorating flavor. This dish makes hot and humid weather something to look forward to.

71

Fedelini with Crab and Cabbage

Ingredients (Serves 2)
6 oz (160) fedelini
3 3/4 oz (110 g) canned crab
1/4 head cabbage
1 clove garlic
1 Tbsp olive oil
Salt and pepper, to taste

Instructions
1. Cut cabbage into bite-size pieces. Mince garlic.
2. Start boiling pasta in salted water. Set timer for 30 seconds to 1 minute less than time indicated by package directions.
3. Add olive oil to a heated pan and sauté garlic over low heat until lightly browned. Add canned crab meat along with canning liquid.

4. Add cabbage to boiling pasta 20 seconds before timer goes off. Drain pasta and cabbage and add to sauce in pan. Season to taste with salt and pepper.

Note
- Do not overcook cabbage. If using soft, spring cabbage, shred thinly and add it to pasta after boiling. It'll be cooked by the steam from the hot noodles.
- This recipe also works well with canned tuna or canned scallops.

Spaghetti with Potato and Basil

Ingredients (Serves 2)
6 oz (160) spaghetti
1 potato, peeled
3 Tbsp pine nuts
12 fresh basil leaves
3 cloves garlic
2 Tbsp olive oil
Salt and pepper, to taste
Freshly grated parmesan cheese, to taste

Instructions
1. Cut potato into thin rectangular bars and soak in water for 3 minutes. Toast pine nuts in a toaster oven until golden brown. Mince basil and garlic.
2. Start boiling pasta in salted water. Set timer for 1 minute less than time indicated by package directions.
3. Add olive oil to a heated pan. Drain potatoes and cook on high heat until lightly browned. Add garlic and sauté until fragrant. Add basil and sauté. Add 1 1/2 ladlefuls of pasta broth.
4. When timer goes off, drain pasta and stir into sauce in pan. Season to taste with salt and pepper. Serve in dishes and use a peeler to garnish with parmesan cheese shavings. Sprinkle with extra olive oil and top with roasted pine nuts.

Capellini with Eggplant and Anchovies

Ingredients (Serves 2)

6 oz (160) capellini
2 eggplants (the small Italian or Japanese variety)
1 tomato
10 black olives, pitted
3 anchovies
A ⎡ grated garlic
  ⎣ 2 Tbsp olive oil
1 1/2 Tbsp olive oil
Salt and pepper, to taste
Lemon

Instructions

1. Peel eggplants and cut lengthwise into 6 pieces. Soak in salted water for 3 minutes. Dice tomato into 1/3" (7 mm) cubes. Mince olives and anchovies.

2. Add olive oil to a heated pan and stir-fry eggplants over high heat until browned. Set aside in a bowl. Add tomato, olive, anchovies and mixture A to bowl and mix.

3. Boil pasta in salted water for slightly longer than time indicated by package directions. Rinse and chill in ice water. Drain pasta well and add to bowl from step 2. Season to taste with salt and pepper. Add a squeeze or two of lemon and mix again. Sprinkle with extra olive oil, if desired.

Note
- Peel eggplants for a tender texture that goes well with fine capellini noodles.
- Chilled pasta does not absorb flavor very well, so add plenty of salt when boiling noodles. Cook noodles until soft, keeping in mind they become firm again when chilled in ice water.

Spinach Lasagna
Creamy lasagna without white sauce

Making lasagna is a chore if you have to prepare both meat sauce and white sauce. So I don't bother with the white sauce. And I'm not just being lazy, mind you. Lasagna made with fresh cream has a deliciously mellow flavor that's not too strong and keeps you coming back for more.

Salmon and Penne au Gratin

Crispy salmon gives this gratin a delicious flavor.

Start with getting those fish good and cooked. Crisped-on-the-outside salmon is essential to making a flavorful dish, so don't hold back. This dish also makes good use of al dente penne.

Thin Japanese Noodles

Thin Japanese *somen* and *hiyamugi* noodles are usually eaten chilled,
but you can enjoy them as *nyumen* (warm noodles) in soups, too.
As with other noodles, boil them for slightly less than the time indicated by package directions.
In the case of *somen* and *hiyamugi*, however, the boiling time is short to start with,
so it is difficult to be specific about cooking times. But there's no need to worry too much,
as the noodles firm up again when chilled in ice water.
Usually additional cold water is added to control boiling
when cooking thin noodles, but this is not always necessary.
I boil my noodles with the heat adjusted to keep the water at a low boil.
Therefore, I don't need to use cooling water.
Either way, the most important thing with thin Japanese noodles is
rinsing them thoroughly after boiling.
Rinse away any excess starch for deliciously smooth noodles.

Somen with Mixed Tempura

Well-chilled noodles and crispy crunchy tempura!

Tempura should be fried slowly to allow the natural moisture to evaporate. That way you get deliciously crunchy tempura that stays crisp even after being dipped in sauce. Tender, crispy tempura, tangled up in thin, chilled noodles. No words can truly describe it, but I'll try: "Yum."

Somen with Mixed Tempura

Ingredients (Serves 2)

5 1/4 oz (150 g) *somen* noodles (or vermicelli)
1/2 bunch molokheiya (Egyptian spinach. Or spinach)
1/2 onion
5 1/4 oz (150 g) shelled shrimp
Batter
⌐ 1 C flour
│ 1/2 to 2/3 C water
└ Pinch salt
Flour for coating
Oil for deep frying
1 2/3 C noodle sauce (*men tsuyu*), diluted to taste
Chopped spring onions (or scallions), roasted white sesame seeds and grated ginger, to taste

1 Make Tempura

1. Use only the leaves of the molokheiya (or spinach). Thinly slice onion lengthwise.

2. Devein shrimp and coat in flour.

3. Combine batter ingredients and mix well. The consistency should be close to this.

4. Divide batter into 3 separate bowls. Dredge molokheiya, onion, and shrimp separately. Coat well.

5. Heat oil to 320°F (160°C). Start by frying molokheiya. Scoop up with a spatula and gently slide into oil.

6. Let fry over medium low heat undisturbed until crispy. Turn over and continue frying slowly until batter is crispy. Set aside.

2 Prepare Noodles

7. Next fry onion. Scoop up with a spatula and slide into hot oil. Fry over medium high heat until crispy.

8. Finally, fry shrimp over high heat until crispy.

9. Add *somen* to boiling water and adjust heat to keep water at a gently rolling boil without allowing it to boil over. No cooling water is necessary.

10. Rinse thoroughly.

11. Chill noodles in ice water. Drain and serve in bowls. Serve tempura and condiments in separate dishes and serve with well-chilled noodle sauce (*men tsuyu*).

Somen Scramble

Use *awamori* liquor for an authentic flavor

This is the ultimate stamina-building *somen* noodle recipe—Okinawan power. If the noodles stick to the pan don't hesitate to dig in and pry them off. They're good even when crunchy. So don't worry, be happy, and enjoy this delicious dish from the southern islands of Japan.

Ingredients (Serves 2)

5 1/4 oz (150 g) *somen* noodles
　(or vermicelli)
3 1/2 oz (100 g) ground pork
1 bunching onion (or green onion or leek)
1/2 bunch garlic chives
1/2 bag bean sprouts
1 egg, lightly beaten
1 clove garlic, minced
1 nub ginger, minced
1 Tbsp sesame oil
1 to 2 Tbsp *awamori*
　(distilled rice
　liqueur. Or sake)
1 tsp soy sauce
1 to 2 pinches sugar
Salt, pepper, cayenne
　pepper and rice
　vinegar, to taste

Note

- Coat pan well with oil
　to keep noodles from sticking. (See page 34)
- If you turn heat down to low before adding
　somen noodles, you don't have to rush when
　loosening them up in the pan. If it looks like
　they're sticking, add a little more oil.

1. Slice bunching onion diagonally. Cut garlic chives to 2" (5 cm) lengths. Remove root ends of bean sprouts.

2. Boil *somen* noodles, rinse thoroughly and drain.

3. Add sesame oil to a heated pan and sauté ginger and garlic over low heat until fragrant. Add ground pork and stir-fry over high heat.

4. When meat is browned add bunching onion and stir-fry until lightly browned.

5. Add bean sprouts and stir-fry. When sprouts are cooked through add *somen* noodles, pulling apart in the pan.

6. Stir, combining noodles and ingredients. Move noodle mixture to one side and add lightly beaten egg to the other.

7. Scramble egg until half-cooked, then mix into noodles.

8. Add garlic chives and stir quickly. Add *awamori*, soy sauce, and sugar. Stir. Season with salt and pepper.

9 Finish with rice vinegar and cayenne pepper.

Hot Soymilk *Somen* Noodles with Clams

Clams and soymilk are a smooth combination!

Slowly simmer freshwater clams in a bath of soymilk.
The result is a deliciously mellow soup with a rich and creamy flavor.
Add oyster sauce for an extra boost.

Ingredients (Serves 2)

5 1/4 oz (150 g) *somen* noodles (or vermicelli)
10 1/2 oz (300 g) freshwater (*shijimi*) clams, soaked to remove sand
2 1/4 C soymilk
2 Tbsp sake
1/2 Tbsp oyster sauce
1 nub ginger, grated
Chopped scallions
Aonori dried seaweed, to taste
Salt and pepper, to taste

Note

Avoid bringing soymilk to a rolling boil or it will separate. Keep at a low boil.

1. Rub clams together and rinse well. Place in pot and add sake. Cook over medium heat.

2. Pour in soymilk when clamshells open. Simmer for 5 minutes over low heat.

3. Stir in oyster sauce. Season to taste with salt.

4. Boil *somen* noodles, rinse thoroughly, and drain.

5. Add noodles to clam soup to reheat. Stir in grated ginger. Serve in bowls and top with chopped spring onions and seaweed. Finish with pepper.

Nyumen
Use light soy sauce

Hot *somen* noodles are called *nyumen*, and are best served simply. Lean chicken meat, light soy sauce, *mitsuba* and *yuzu* peel all serve to contribute a classy quality.

Ingredients (Serves 2)
5 1/4 oz (150 g) *somen* noodles (or vermicelli)
3 1/2 oz (100 g) chicken breast
4 slices grilled fish cake (*yaki-kamaboko*) 1/8"
   thick (or sub. imitation crab stick, sautéed)
Mitsuba (or watercress or chervil)
Yuzu peel, julienned (or sub. lemon zest)
3 C Japanese soup broth
   (see Reference Guide)
1/2 Tbsp each light soy sauce and mirin
   (sweet cooking wine)
Salt, to taste
Roasted white sesame seeds, to taste

Instructions
1. Slice chicken breast into 1/5" (5 mm) wide strips and grilled fish cake into thin strips. Cut *mitsuba* to 1 1/4" (3 cm) pieces. For soup broth, bonito flavor works best.
2. Add chicken to boiling soup broth and simmer for 5 to 7 minutes. Stir in light soy sauce and mirin. Season with salt, adding gradually until flavor is just right.
3. Boil *somen* noodles for slightly less than time indicated by package directions and rinse well. Drain and add to soup pot, cooking just long enough to reheat noodles. Serve in bowls and top with fish cake, *mitsuba*, and *yuzu* peel. Finish with roasted sesame seeds.

Sticky *Hiyamugi*

Just mix and eat!

Get a bunch of gooey ingredients and mix it all up. The amount doesn't matter: add as much as you like of whatever you want. Use *hiyamugi*, not *somen*. *Hiyamugi* is thicker and able to hold its own under all those ingredients.

Ingredients (Serves 2)

5 1/4 oz (150 g) *hiyamugi* noodles
2 packs *natto* (fermented soybeans)
4 to 5 okra
2/5 C Japanese yam (*yamaimo*), grated
Nametake (or enoki) mushrooms, to taste
Chopped spring onions (or scallions), to taste
Dash roasted white sesame seeds
1 2/3 C noodle sauce (*men tsuyu*),
   diluted to taste
Toasted nori seaweed, to taste

Instructions

1. Blanch okra, remove stems, and slice into rounds. Add all ingredients other than toasted nori seaweed and noodles to noodle sauce and stir.
2. Boil *hiyamugi* noodles and rinse thoroughly. Chill in ice water and drain. Serve in bowls and top with sauce from step 1. Serve with toasted nori seaweed on the side.

Somen with Chilled Sesame Sauce

Whip up authentic flavor with a blender!

I used to believe that grinding sesame seeds with a mortar and pestle was the only proper way to make chilled sesame sauce. But one day I tried throwing it all into a blender. It was ready in a snap—and very tasty. So, I recommend using a blender. Of course, if you still think using a mortar and pestle is the only right way to do it, be my guest.

Ingredients (Serves 2)

5 1/4 oz (150 g) *somen* noodles (or vermicelli)
1 1/4 C Japanese soup broth (see Reference Guide)
1 dried mackerel (*aji*)
1/2 cucumber
1 eggplant (the small Japanese or Italian variety)
1 bud red Japanese ginger (*myoga*)
6 *shiso* leaves (or basil or mint)
2 to 3 Tbsp roasted white sesame seeds
1 Tbsp miso
Salt and grated ginger, to taste

Instructions

1. Chill soup broth in the refrigerator. Grill dried mackerel until slightly charred and set aside to cool. Remove head and bones from fish and add fish meat to blender. Slice cucumber and eggplant into thin rounds and place in a bowl. Rub 2 to 3 pinches of salt into cucumber and eggplant. Julienne ginger and shiso.

2. Add roasted sesame seeds, miso, and half of chilled soup broth to blender. Blend until mixture is a smooth paste. Add remaining soup broth and blend again. Add salt as needed (the flavor should be slightly strong). Squeeze excess liquid from eggplants and cucumbers and add to sesame sauce.

3. Cook *somen* noodles in boiling water and rinse thoroughly. Chill in ice water, drain, and serve in bowls. Pour sesame sauce from step 2 over noodles and garnish as desired with shiso, ginger, and sesame seeds.

Asian Dipping Noodles
Packs a spicy punch!

Dip chilled noodles into piping hot coconut curry sauce. The slick noodles in this rich sauce will energize you. Use Thai fish sauce for genuine flavor. If it's too fishy for you, soy sauce and salt are both acceptable substitutes. And of course, adding cilantro is up to you.

Ingredients (Serves 2)

5 1/4 oz (150 g) *somen* noodles
5 1/4 oz (150 g) pork belly, thinly sliced
1/2 red bell pepper
2 cloves garlic
2 nubs ginger
1 Tbsp sesame oil
2 red chili peppers
1 Tbsp sake

2 tsp curry powder
14 oz (400 g) coconut milk, canned
A ⎡ 2 Tbsp Nam pla (Thai fish sauce)
  ⎣ 1 Tbsp each sugar and oyster sauce
Salt, to taste
Fresh cilantro, chopped
Chopped spring onions (or scallions)

Instructions

1. Cut pork into bite-size pieces. Cut red bell pepper in half widthwise then julienne lengthwise. Mince garlic and ginger.
2. Add sesame oil to a heated pan and sauté ginger and garlic over low heat. Remove stems from chili peppers and cut into rounds with scissors right into the pan. When oil is fragrant add pork and stir-fry over high heat until browned. Add bell peppers and stir-fry.
3. Stir in sake and curry powder. Add coconut milk and simmer for 1 minute over medium low heat. Add mixture A and stir. Season to taste with salt.
4. Boil *somen* noodles and rinse thoroughly. Chill in ice water, drain and serve in dishes. Pour dipping sauce into bowls and add cilantro and spring onions on the side.

Hiyamugi with Pork and Sesame Sauce

Rich sauce is delicious and filling!

Hiyamugi noodles are thin but toothsome. I have been a big fan of these noodles since I was a child, but for some reason they are not as well known as *somen* noodles. They may be hard to find and are often only sold in summer, but do your best. I sincerely hope that someday *hiyamugi* will get the acclaim it deserves. Enjoy them with pork, sesame sauce and plenty of condiments.

Ingredients (Serves 2)

5 1/4 oz (150 g) *hiyamugi* noodles
5 1/4 oz (150 g) pork shoulder, thinly sliced
1/2 bag string beans
10 *shiso* leaves
2" (5 cm) bunching onion (or leek)
2 1/2 C noodle sauce (*men tsuyu*),
    diluted to taste
2 Tbsp white sesame paste
2 Tbsp ground black sesame seeds
Grated ginger, to taste

Instructions

1. Cut pork into bite-size pieces. Remove stems of string beans and chop into small pieces. Mince *shiso* leaves. Slice bunching onion into thin rounds.
2. Bring water to a boil in a pot and add salt. Add string beans and boil for about 20 seconds. Set aside. Add pork to boiling water, cook until browned, and set aside. Add all ingredients (except leek and noodles) to a bowl and mix.
3. Cook *hiyamugi* noodles in boiling water and rinse thoroughly. Chill in ice water, drain, and serve in dishes. Serve sauce in a separate dish and top with bunching onion.

Bibim Guksu

**Sweet, sour, and spicy,
with luxurious beef**

This is a Korean spicy noodle dish that
uses *somen*. It uses rich beef ribs, but
thanks to the sweet and sour sauce it's
very balanced. The amount of daikon kimchi, gochujang and rice vinegar you use is
up to you. Any amount will be delicious.

Ingredients (Serves 2)

5 1/4 oz (150 g) *somen* noodles
5 1/4 oz (150 g) boneless beef rib (*galbi*)
1 cucumber
1 3/4 oz (50 g) daikon kimchi (*ggakdugi*)
1/2 Tbsp sesame oil
A ⎡ 1 Tbsp each sake and soy sauce
  ⎣ 1/2 Tbsp sugar
Chopped spring onions (or scallions)
  ⎡ 1 1/2 Tbsp each sesame oil and soy sauce
  ⎢ 1 Tbsp each rice vinegar and ground white
  ⎢   sesame seeds
B ⎢ 1/2 Tbsp gochujang (Korean chili paste)
  ⎣ 1 tsp sugar

Instructions

1. Slice beef into thin strips. Peel cucumbers,
   cut in half lengthwise then into 1/8" (3 mm)
   half-circle slices. Mince daikon kimchi.
2. Add sesame oil to a heated pan and stir-fry
   beef over high heat until browned. Add
   mixture A and coat well. Combine beef,
   cucumber, daikon kimchi, spring onions and
   mixture B in a bowl.
3. Boil *somen* noodles and rinse thoroughly.
   Chill in ice water, drain, and add to sauce in
   bowl from step 2. Stir well and serve. Add
   additional sesame oil, if desired, and add
   extra gochujang on the side.

Celery and Bell Pepper Marinade

Refreshingly sour and deliciously crunchy. Great with rich noodle dishes!

Ingredients (Serves 4)
2 stalks celery
1 red bell pepper

A ⎰ 3 to 4 Tbsp rice vinegar
  ⎪ 1 Tbsp olive oil
  ⎪ 1/2 tsp dried basil
  ⎪ 3 pinches salt
  ⎪ Pinch sugar
  ⎱ Dash pepper

Instructions
1. Peel celery and slice into bite-size sticks. Cut bell pepper into strips.
2. Combine mixture A in a bowl and stir well. Add ingredients from step 1 and add celery leaves, mix well and chill in refrigerator. You may also marinate vegetables by adding all ingredients to a plastic bag and shaking to coat. It's ready to eat after about 20 minutes.

Grilled Scallop Carpaccio

Sweet and roasted grilled scallops whet the appetite for pasta!

Ingredients (Serves 2 to 4)
4 fresh scallops
1 1/2 Tbsp olive oil
Salt, pepper and lemon juice, to taste
Italian parsley, chopped

Instructions
1. Cut scallops to half of original thickness.
2. Add 1 Tbsp olive oil to a heated pan and sauté scallops on high heat until both sides are lightly browned. Serve on dishes and finish with remaining olive oil, salt, pepper, and lemon juice. Garnish with Italian parsley.

Plum Tomato and Camembert Cheese Salad

Fresh tomato and rich cheese— delicious with any noodle dish

Ingredients (Serves 2)
2 small plum tomatoes
1/4 round Camembert cheese
2 Tbsp minced onion

A ⎰ Dash grated garlic
  ⎪ 1/2 Tbsp rice vinegar
  ⎪ 2 pinches salt
  ⎪ Pinch sugar
  ⎪ Dash pepper
  ⎱ 1 Tbsp olive oil

Instructions
1. Soak minced onion for 3 minutes in water and drain well. Cut tomato and cheese into bite-size chunks.
2. Combine mixture A and drained onion in a bowl.
3. Serve tomato and cheese in dishes and top with dressing from step 2.

Milk Jelly

Sweet bean paste is a great match for the mild flavor of this Japanese gelatin

Ingredients (Serves 2 to 4)
4/5 C milk
3 Tbsp condensed milk
A ⎡ 1/15 oz (2 g) powdered agar-agar
⎢ (*kanten*. Or powdered gelatin)
⎣ 2/5 C boiling water
Sweet red bean paste, to taste

Instructions
1. Combine mixture A and stir thoroughly.
2. In a bowl, combine milk, condensed milk and agar-agar mixture and stir well. Pour mixture into a square mold and chill in refrigerator until firm (about 1 hour). Cut into bite-size cubes and top with sweet red bean paste.

Strawberry Yogurt Jelly

Delicious, creamy, and a welcome treat after any noodle dish!

Ingredients (Serves 2 to 4)
1 1/5 C plain yogurt
2 1/2 Tbsp strawberry jam
2 to 3 Tbsp sugar
A ⎡ 3/16 oz 5 g powdered gelatin
⎣ 1/5 C boiling water

Instructions
1. Combine mixture A and stir thoroughly.
2. Combine yogurt, jam and sugar in a bowl and mix well. Add gelatin mixture from step 1, straining through a mesh or tea strainer, and stir. Pour into small dishes and chill in refrigerator until firm (about 2 hours).

Tea Jelly with Lemon Syrup

Refreshing and mildly sweet. The perfect dessert after rich noodles!

Ingredients (Serves 2 to 4)
1 1/5 C strong tea
3 Tbsp sugar
A ⎡ 3/16 oz (5 g) powdered gelatin
⎣ 1/5 C boiled water
Lemon syrup ⎡ Juice from 1/2 lemon
⎢ 1/5 C water
⎣ 4 Tbsp sugar

Instructions
1. Combine mixture A and stir thoroughly.
2. Combine tea and sugar in a bowl and stir well. Add gelatin mixture from step 1, straining through a mesh or tea strainer, and stir. Pour into small dishes and chill in refrigerator until firm, for about 2 hours.
3. Make syrup: heat water and sugar in a pan until sugar melts. When sugar is completely melted add lemon juice and stir. Move to a bowl and chill in refrigerator until chilled.
4. Serve jelly in dishes and top with syrup.

Note
You can use milk or condensed milk in place of lemon syrup.

Little Sweets

Kentaro Kobayashi

Born 1972 in Tokyo, Japan. Began working as an illustrator while attending Musashino College of Fine Arts. With a motto of "Easy and delicious, stylish yet realistic," Kentaro began displaying his creativity and outstanding cooking sense in magazines and television appearances shortly after. As a popular culinary artist representing the younger generation, he proposes delicious yet accessible dishes with energy and flair. This book is a collection of his favorite noodle recipes, filled with both original ideas and well preserved classics, all in keeping with his motto. You can also see the influence of his mother, the famous culi-

in

Noodle Comfort

Translation: Patricia Kawasaki
Vetting: Lisa Reilly

Copyright © 2009 by Kentaro Kobayashi
Photography © 2009 by Hideo Sawai

All rights reserved.

Published by Vertical, Inc., New York.

Originally published in Japanese as *Kentarono Men* by Bunka Shuppankyoku, Tokyo, 2006.

ISBN 978-1-934287-57-6

Manufactured in The United States of America

First American Edition

Vertical, Inc.
www.vertical-inc.com